D1152849

Humour £2-50

⑩

Happy Birthday

love Tim

& Dave xx.

Also by Nigel Rees
'Quote . . . Unquote'
Graffiti Lives, OK
Very Interesting . . . But Stupid!
Graffiti 2

NIGEL REES

— PRESENTS —

" THE QUOTE...UNQUOTE "

BOOK OF

LOVE, DEATH

AND THE

UNIVERSE

WITH ILLUSTRATIONS BY MICHAEL FFOLKES

London

GEORGE ALLEN & UNWIN

Boston   Sydney

First published in 1980

This book is copyright under the Berne Convention. All rights are reserved. Apart from any fair dealing for the purpose of private study, research, criticism or review, as permitted under the Copyright Act, 1956, no part of this publication may be reproduced, stored in a retrieval system, or transmitted, in any form or by any means, electronic, electrical, chemical, mechanical, optical, photocopying, recording or otherwise, without the prior permission of the copyright owner. Enquiries should be sent to the publishers at the undermentioned address:

GEORGE ALLEN & UNWIN LTD
40 Museum Street, London WC1A 1LU

This edition ©Nigel Rees Productions Ltd 1980

Illustrations ©Michael ffolkes 1980

British Library Cataloguing in Publication Data

Rees, Nigel
    Nigel Rees presents the 'quote-unquote'
    book of love, death and the universe.
    1. Quotations, English
    2. 'Quote-unquote' book of love, death
and the universe
808.88'2   PN6081   80-40108

ISBN 0-04-827022-9

Art Director David Pocknell
Design Michael Cavers

Set in 10pt Sabon Compugraphic
Printed and bound in Great Britain by
William Clowes (Beccles) Limited
Beccles and London

Contents

Preface

As it happens, D H Lawrence was not writing about *Love, Death and the Universe* when he encountered, 'nothing but old fags and cabbage-stumps of quotations from the Bible and the rest, stewed in the juice of deliberate journalistic dirty-mindedness' -he was talking about the works of James Joyce. Nevertheless, that will do very nicely to describe this second volume -part anthology and part quiz- book - published under the *'Quote . . . Unquote'* banner. I, too, have been foraging in the Bible and some other rather less wholesome places to produce a volume which is as wide-ranging, if not quite as all-embracing, as its title suggests.

The radio programme *Quote . . . Unquote* was first broadcast by the BBC in January 1976. From the start I decided that the quiz should not be limited to famous quotations from the conventional sources of literature and politics, but should range over all areas of writing and reported speech. Hence my inclusion of catchphrases, graffiti, and what I call 'eavesdroppings' - peculiar things overheard. These last two areas brought an enormous audience response. As a result, the programme has become as much an anthology as a quiz.

This broad sweep has been reflected too in the first anthology, *'Quote . . .Unquote'*; *Graffiti Lives, OK*; and, *Very Interesting . . . But Stupid!* (a survey of show- business catchphrases).

Now, for your enjoyment, here is *Love, Death and the Universe*. It is based largely on material used in the third, fourth and fifth series of the radio programme, but also contains some material which could never have been broadcast over the air. My own stock of favourite quotations, old and new, has been topped up by many, many helpful listeners and by those who took part in the broadcasts themselves, namely:

Kingsley Amis; George Axelrod; Joan Bakewell; Malcolm Bradbury; Tina Brown; John Bird; Richard Boston; Rob Buckman; James Burke; Denise Coffey; Peter Cook; Barry Cryer; Russell Davies; Ronald Fletcher; Anna Ford; Terence Frisby; Clement Freud; Graeme Garden; Patrick Garland; Prunella Gee; Lord George-Brown; Jacky Gillott; Richard Gordon; Benny Green; Germaine Greer; Celia Haddon; Roy Hudd; Richard Ingrams; P D James; Martin Jarvis; Brian Johnston; Peter Jones; P J Kavanagh; Neil Kinnock; Robert Lacey; Ann Leslie; Henry Livings; Arthur Marshall; Christopher Matthew; Ian McKellen; George Mikes; Spike Milligan; John Mortimer; Malcolm Muggeridge; Derek Parker; Molly Parkin; Peter Porter; Hilary Pritchard; William Rushton; Norma Shepherd; Richard Stilgoe; John Taylor; Leslie Thomas; Dick Vosburgh -and not forgetting the programme's two successive producers, John Lloyd and Geoffrey Perkins. To all these people, I offer my thanks.

I hope the book proves that, as Ratty might have said, there is *nothing* - absolutely nothing - half so much worth doing as simply messing about with quotations.

I Loved Kirk So Much . . . !

'What is Love?' asked Jesting Pilate; and would not stay for an answer. Joyce McKinney thought she knew. In 1977, the former Miss Wyoming was charged in an English court with kidnapping Kirk Anderson, a Mormon missionary and her ex-lover. She allegedly abducted Mr Anderson to a remote country cottage where he was chained to the bed and forced to make love to her. 'I loved Kirk so much,' Miss McKinney declared to a stunned court, 'I would have skied down Mount Everest in the nude with a carnation up my nose.'

For more devastating insights concerning the nature of Love, Sex and Marriage, read on! See also the chapter entitled *Four Legs Good, Two Legs Bad.*

I have made love to ten thousand women.

> *Georges Simenon, creator of Maigret (when asked if he was sure this figure was correct, he said: 'Yes, I went back and checked.')*

Sex is the gateway to life.

> *Frank Harris to Enid Bagnold*

So I went through the gateway in an upper room at the Café Royal.

> *Enid Bagnold*

Called to see you but you were in.

> *Note allegedly left by Karl Miller who, when a Cambridge undergraduate, called on a friend and found him in flagrante.*

I want a sense of purpose in my life. I don't want to die in Chelsea with my knickers down.

> *Character in Jilly Cooper's Emily*

The pleasure is momentary, the position ridiculous, and the expense damnable.

> *Fourth Earl of Chesterfield*
> (1694-1773)

Sexual intercourse began
In nineteen sixty-three
(which was rather late for me) -
Between the end of the Chatterley Ban
And the Beatles' first LP.

> *Philip Larkin,* Annus Mirabilis

'Pray, my dear,' quoth my mother, 'have you not forgot to wind up the clock?' - 'Good G--!' cried my father, making an exclamation, but taking care to moderate his voice at the same time, - 'Did ever woman, since the creation of the world, interrupt a man with such a silly question?'

> *Laurence Sterne,* Tristram
> Shandy

Well, you see, my dears, the one in front is blind and her friend is pushing her all the way to St Dunstan's.

> *Noel Coward, on being asked*
> *by young friends what two*
> *dogs were doing together.*

Well, did you do any fornicating this weekend?

> *Richard Nixon attempting*
> *smalltalk with David Frost at*
> *the time of their TV*
> *interviews, 1977*

Friar Barnadine: Thou hast committed — —
Barabas: Fornication: but that was in another country;
       And beside the wench is dead.

> *Marlowe,* The Jew of Malta

'Come, Come,' said Tom's father, 'at your time of life,
There's no longer excuse for this playing the rake -
It is time you should think, boy, of taking a wife' -
'Why, so it is, father - whose wife shall I take?'

> *Thomas Moore,* A Joke
> Versified

Tell him I've been too fucking busy - or vice versa.

Dorothy Parker

There, but for a typographical error is the story of my life.

Dorothy Parker, when told at a Hallowe'en party that people were ducking for apples.

My Lord (the first Earl of Sandwich) told me that among his father's many old sayings that he had writ in a book of his, this is one: that he that doth get a wench with child and marries her afterward, it is as if a man should shit in his hat and then clap it upon his head.

Samuel Pepys, Diary, 7 October 1660

One time getting one of the Mayds of Honour up against a tree in a Wood . . . who seemed at first boarding to be somewhat fearfull of her Honour, and modest, she cryed, sweet Sir Walter, what doe you me ask? Will you undoe me? Nay, sweet Sir Walter! Sweet Sir Walter! Sir Walter! At last, as the danger and the pleasure at the same time grew higher, she cryed in extasey, Swisser Swatter, Swisser Swatter.

John Aubrey on Sir Walter Raleigh

And so to Mrs Martin and there did what je voudrais avec her, both devante and backward, which is also muy bon plazer.

Pepys again, 4 June 1666

Some things can't be ravished. You can't ravish a tin of sardines.

D H Lawrence, Lady Chatterley's Lover

It's impossible to ravish me / I'm so willing.

John Fletcher, The Faithful Shepherdess, *III.i (1610)*

Whatever Turns You On

You are an A.1 tumble-bun.

phrase designed to increase feminine fervour, suggested by John Eichenlaub, MD, in The Marriage Art

The trouble with Ian is that he gets off with women because he can't get on with them.

Rosamond Lehmann on Ian Fleming

She had remarkably lively eyes, but so small they were almost invisible when she laughed; and a foot, the least of any woman in England.

contemporary description of Nell Gwyn, mistress of Charles II

'That's my foot . . . it's the handsomest foot in all Paris. There's only one in all Paris to match it, and here it is,' and she laughed heartily (like a merry peal of bells) and stuck out the other.

George du Maurier, Trilby

I'll come no more behind your scenes, David; for the silk stockings and white bosoms of your actresses excite my amorous propensities.

Samuel Johnson to David Garrick

Give a man a free hand and he'll run it all over you.

Mae West

Long-legged girls are fascinating - built for walking through grass.

Laurie Lee

British boobs are the best in the world.

Mrs Jane Contour (sic), bra expert

The artist has won through his fantasy what before he could only win *in* his fantasy: honour, power, and the love of women.

Sigmund Freud, Introductory Lectures on Psycho-Analysis, No. 23

She is a very fascinating woman. And he is very fond of fascinating with her.

Samuel Butler

It is not necessary to allege that a girl is under 21 years of age, because all girls are under 21 - although females may be women at the age of 18.

Section 23, British Sexual Offences Act, 1953

The Twist is a perpendicular expression of a horizontal desire.

Anon

The trouble with nude dancing is that not everything stops when the music stops.

Sir Robert Helpmann

"Call Me Ishmael"

Authors probably spend more time agonising over their first sentences than over any other part of their books. Like Herman Melville's opening to *Moby Dick* ('Call Me Ishmael'), the first sentence should at the very least buttonhole the reader. At best, it can encapsulate the flavour of what is to come. Of what books are these the first sentences? The answers are over the page.

1

If you really want to hear about it, the first thing you'll probably want to know is where I was born, and what my lousy childhood was like, and how my parents were occupied and all before they had me, and all that David Copperfield kind of crap.

2

It was a bright cold day in April, and the clocks were striking 13.

3

It is a truth universally acknowledged, that a single man in possession of a good fortune, must be in want of a wife.

4

In the name of God, the most merciful, the most compassionate.

5

The human race, to which so many of my readers belong.

6

Last night I dreamt I went to Manderley again.

7

The scene and smoke and sweat of a casino are nauseating
at three in the morning.

8

I can see by my watch, without taking my hand from the
left grip of the cycle, that it is eight-thirty in the morning.

9

It was the best of times, it was the worst of times, it was the
age of wisdom, it was the age of foolishness, it was the
epoch of belief, it was the epoch of incredulity, it was the
season of light, it was the season of darkness, it was the
spring of hope, it was the winter of despair.

10

I am a camera with its shutter open, quite passive,
recording, not thinking.

Answers
Call Me Ishmael

1
J D Salinger *The Catcher in the Rye*

2
George Orwell *1984*

3
Jane Austen *Pride and Prejudice*

4
The Koran

5
G K Chesterton *The Napoleon of Notting Hill*

6
Daphne du Maurier *Rebecca*

7
Ian Fleming *Casino Royale*

8
Robert M Pirsig *Zen and the Art of Motorcyle Maintenance*

9
Charles Dickens *A Tale of Two Cities*

10
Christopher Isherwood, 'A Berlin Diary', *Goodbye to Berlin*

That Title From A Better Man I Stole* - 1

Few authors have surpassed Aldous Huxley in the number of quotations they have used as titles for their books. Quite apart from *Antic Hay* (Marlowe, *Edward II*) and *Brave New World* (Shakespeare, *The Tempest*), the majority of his works have titles taken mostly from Shakespeare. Where do these titles come from? The answers are over the page.

1
After Many a Summer Dies the Swan

2
Beyond the Mexique Bay

3
Brief Candles

4
Eyeless in Gaza

5
Jesting Pilate

6
Mortal Coils

7
Those Barren Leaves

8
Time Must Have a Stop

---

* R L Stevenson

Answers
That Title From A Better Man
I Stole

1

Tennyson, *Tithonus:* 'The woods decay, the woods decay and fall,/ The vapours weep their burthen to the ground,/ Man comes and tills the field and lies beneath,/ And after many a summer dies the swan.'

2

Andrew Marvell, *Bermudas:* 'Echo beyond the Mexique Bay.'

3

Shakespeare, *Macbeth* V.v: 'Out, out, brief candle!'

4

Milton, *Samson Agonistes:* 'Eyeless in Gaza, at the mill with slaves.'

5

Bacon, *Essays (Of Truth):* 'What is truth? said jesting Pilate; and would not stay for an answer.'

6

Shakespeare, *Hamlet* III.i: 'When we have shuffled off this mortal coil.'

7

Wordsworth, *The Tables Turned:* 'Enough of science and of art;/ Close up these barren leaves;/ Come forth, and bring with you a heart/ That watches and receives.'

8

Shakespeare, *King Henry IV,* Part I, V.iv: 'And time, that takes survey of all the world,/ Must have a stop.'

Hell Hath No Fury Like A Woman's Corns

'Hanging is too good for a man who makes puns,' said Fred Allen. 'He should be drawn and quoted.' The following are all well-known sayings which have fallen victim to punsters and word-players. What is the original saying in each case? The answers are on page 22.

1

You cannot serve cod and gammon.

2

Procreation is the thief of time.

3

Every crowd has a silver lining.

4

A consommé devoutly to be wished.

5

Life, Liberty and the Happiness of Pursuit.

6

To err is human, to er-er-er is unforgivable.

7

O Klemperer, O mores!

8

And the meek shall inhibit the earth.

9

Streak now or for ever hold your piece.

10

The price of liberty is eternal violence.

11

Is this the face that shipped a thousand lunches?

12

Every member of the orchestra carries a conductor's baton
in his knapsack.

13

Speak softly and own a big, mean Dobermann.

14

Alas, poor Yorlik, I knew him
backwards.

Answers
Nor Hell A Fury Like A Woman Scorned

1

'Ye cannot serve God and mammon' - St Matthew 6:24

2

'Procrastination is the thief of time' - Edward Young, *The Complaint: Night Thoughts*

3

'Every cloud had a silver lining' - proverb, altered by P T Barnum

4

'A consummation/Devoutly to be wished' - Shakespeare, *Hamlet,* III.i, altered by Noel Coward

5

'Life, Liberty and the pursuit of happiness' - the American Declaration of Independence

6

'To err is human, to forgive, divine' - Pope, *An Essay on Criticism*

7

'O Tempora, O mores' - Cicero

8

'Blessed are the meek: for they shall inherit the world' - St Matthew 5:3

9

'Let him now speak, or else hereafter for ever hold his peace' - from the Solemnisation of Matrimony in *The Book of Common Prayer*

10

'The condition upon which God hath given liberty to man is
eternal vigilance' - John Philpot Curran, Dublin, 1790 (also
attributed to Thomas Jefferson)

11

'Was this the face that launch'd a thousand ships?'
-Marlowe, *Dr Faustus*

12

'Every French soldier carries in his cartridge-pouch the
baton of a Marshal of France' - attributed to Napoleon,
altered by Tom Stoppard in *Every Good Boy Deserves A
Favour*

13

'Speak softly and carry a big stick' - saying associated with
President Theodore Roosevelt

14

'Alas, poor Yorick . . . I knew him, Horatio' - Shakespeare,
Hamlet, V.i

Sticks And Stones

'Sticks and stones may break my bones,' goes the children's rhyme, 'but words will never hurt me.' One wonders whether the people on the receiving end of these put-downs and squelches would agree . . .

Man at party, effusively: Tallulah! I haven't seen you for forty-one years!
Tallulah Bankhead: I thought I told you to wait in the car.

She was the original good time that was had by all.

> *Bette Davis, of available starlet*

Oh well, you play Bach *your* way. I'll play him *his*.

> *Wanda Landowska, harpsichordist, to fellow musician*

Waldo is one of those people who would be enormously improved by death.

> *Saki,* The Feast of Nemesis

If he didn't exist, it would be unnecessary to invest him.

> *Desmond Elliott on Auberon Waugh*

First bridge player: Well, how would you have played that hand?
Second bridge player: Under an assumed name.

What if the child inherits *my* body and *your* brains?

> *Bernard Shaw to a correspondent who had written: 'You have the greatest brain in the world, and I have the most beautiful body; so we ought to produce the most perfect child.'*

A desiccated calculating machine.

> *Aneurin Bevan's prescription*
> *for the leader of the Labour*
> *Party, 1954, - often taken as*
> *referring to Hugh Gaitskell,*
> *though Bevan denied this*

Actress not noted for her looks: Mr Wilde, you are looking at the ugliest woman in Paris.
Oscar Wilde (flatteringly): In the *world,* madam!

Which part is he playing now?

> *Somerset Maugham watching*
> *Spencer Tracy film* Dr Jekyll
> and Mr Hyde

Nice of you to come, but your head's too small for the camera, you are too thin, and . . . I don't know what it is exactly about the neck . . . but it's not right.

> *Earl St John at Dirk*
> *Bogarde's Rank Organisation*
> *audition*

He's a sort of musical Malcolm Sargent.

> *Sir Thomas Beecham of*
> *Herbert von Karajan*

Rob Buckman, as green young medical student: Just a little prick with a needle.
American patient: I know you are, but what are you going to do?

A Month in the Wrong Country.

> *Noel Coward on an*
> *American production of* The
> Cherry Orchard *set in the*
> *Deep South*

Whenever I see his finger nails, I thank God I don't have to look at his feet.

> *Athene Seyler, actress, on*
> *Hannen Swaffer, journalist*

A man who never missed an occasion to let slip an opportunity.

Bernard Shaw on Lord Roseberry

Bright Young Thing: I liked your book. Who wrote it for you?
Woman writer: I'm glad you enjoyed it. Who read it to you?

Denise Robins: I've just written my 87th book.
Barbara Cartland: I've written 145.
Denise Robins: Oh, I see, one a year.   (attrib)

Not only not a genius, he is intellectually as undistinguished as it is possible to be.

F R Leavis on C P Snow

He has Van Gogh's ear for music.

Orson Welles on Donny Osmond (attrib)

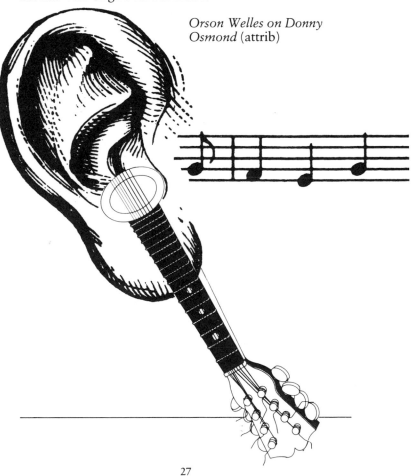

Bessie Braddock, MP: You're drunk!
Winston Churchill: And you, madam, are ugly. But I shall be sober in the morning.

Nancy Astor, MP: If you were my husband, I'd poison your coffee.
Winston Churchill: If you were my wife, I'd drink it.

At social gatherings he was liable to engage in heated and noisy arguments which could ruin a dinner party, and made him the dread of hostesses on both sides of the Atlantic. The tendency was exacerbated by an always generous, and occasionally excessive, alcoholic intake.

> *Obituary of Randolph Churchill in* The Times, *1968*

Dear Randolph, utterly unspoiled by failure.

> *Noel Coward*

In fine, a most excellent person he is and must be allowed for a little conceitedness; but he may well be so; being a man so much above others.

> *Samuel Pepys on John Evelyn*

Marry her! Impossible! You mean a part of her; he could not marry her all himself. There is enough of her to furnish wives for a whole parish. You might people a colony with her; or give an assembly with her; or perhaps take your morning's walk round her, always provided there were frequent resting-places, and you were in rude health.

> *Revd Sydney Smith*

The wriggling ponces of the spoken word.

> *D G Bridson on disc jockeys*

Sylvia Miles would go to the opening of an envelope.

> *Anon*

Oscar Levant (actor-pianist): If you had it all over again, George, would you fall in love with yourself?
George Gershwin: Oscar, why don't you play us a medley of your hit?

Rapacious agent: I was swimming for two hours in shark-infested waters and I got away!
Herman J Manckiewicz (screen writer): I think that's what they call professional courtesy.

Piddling on flannel.

> *Noel Coward on Mozart*

I write as a sow piddles

> *Mozart on Mozart*

Labour MP (of Herbert Morrison): Of course, the trouble with Herbie is - he's his own worst enemy.
Ernest Bevin: Not while I'm alive he ain't.

The only way of deciphering her invitations is to pin them up on the wall and *run* past them.

> *Of Lady Sybil Colefax,*
> *hostess*

Excuse me for interrupting, but I actually thought I heard a line I wrote.

> *George S Kaufman, at*
> *rehearsal for* Animal
> Crackers, *for which he wrote*
> *the script*

Massey won't be satisfied until somebody assassinates him.

> *George S Kaufman on*
> *Raymond Massey's off-stage*
> *interpretation of Abraham*
> *Lincoln*

God finally caught his eye.

> *George S Kaufman, on a dead*
> *waiter*

It makes me want to call out, 'Is there an apple in the house?'

> *C A Lejeune on Charlton*
> *Heston's performance as a*
> *doctor*

Anxious actor: Could you see my wig-join?
Noel Coward: Perfectly, dear boy, perfectly!

I am debarred from putting her in her place - she hasn't got
one.

> *Edith Sitwell, when asked*
> *why she had not put another*
> *writer - who had been rude*
> *-in her place*

Humphrey Bogart's all right until 11.30 pm. After that, the
trouble is, he thinks he's Humphrey Bogart.

> *Dave Chasen,*
> *restaurateur*
> *Hollywood*

Boot Or Bent Toe - Soliloquised The Prince (2,2,2,3,2,2)

No prizes for solving the above crossword puzzle clue.
Indeed, no puzzle to complete with the following clues.
Merely a celebration of memorable crossword clues from a
host of sources - from Torquemada to Ximenes, from *The
Times* to the *New York Times*. The answers
are on page 34.

1
German bowls three out in old people's nursing home (9)

2
More Vivaldi (1,3,3,3,7)

3
Last meal of a drowning mouse (6,3,6)

4
What car is always in neutral? (7)

5
Abbreviations that may be looked up (4-6)

6
For God, for country, and for Yale (10)

7
What do irritated divers do? (4,2,2,7)

8

H, I, J, K, L, M, N, O (5)

9

Citizens likely to rue their ways (9)

10

Heggs (11)

11

The perfect partner (2,5,7)

12

Man in arena to select an entrance (7)

13

Lord, what a dizzy place (12)

14

A poor wicket-keeper, this greybeard loon (3,7,7)

15

Erotic aural experience stimulates attentiveness (5,2,4,4)

16

Official picture of one of the cat's twins (9)

17

View for an orphan (8)

18
I rifle tubs at sea (10)

19
I make-a you a new pair of trousers (9)

20
What Fido does around the tree (4)

21
She's not likely to have children too great for words (9)

22
Did Jack hear them? (9)

23
Scandinavian cat (9)

24
An Irish tart will give you this complaint (9)

<u>Answers</u>
To Be Or Not To Be

1
Geriatric

2
A Man for all Seasons

3
Bubble and squeak

4
Renault

5
Mini-skirts

6
Anticlimax

7
Come up to scratch

8
Water (H to O)

9
Parisians

10
Exasperated

11
An ideal husband (I-deal)

12
Picador

13
Beaconsfield

14
The Ancient Mariner ('who stoppeth one of three')

15
Prick up your ears

16
Identikit

17
Panorama (Pa nor a Ma)

18
Filibuster

19
Euripedes

20
Bark

21
Ineffable

22
Beanstalk

23
Laplander

24
Arthritis

66 <u>Come, Gentlemen, We Sit Too</u> <u>Long on Trifles</u> 99

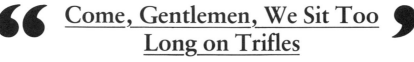

The unfortunate predicament described above (Shakespeare, *Pericles,* II,iii) would surely never have befallen the gentlemen concerned had they consulted the quotation menu printed here. For more bizarre culinary delights, see also *Quote . . . Table d'Hôte.*

If the *soup* had been as warm as the wine, and the wine as old as the fish, and the fish as young as the maid, and the maid as willing as the hostess, it would have been a very good meal.

Anon

Housewarming at Zola's. Very tasty dinner, including some *grouse* whose scented flesh Daudet compared to an old courtesan's flesh marinated in a bidet.

Edmond de Goncourt,
Journal

Tell the cook of this restaurant with my compliments that these are the very worst sandwiches in the whole world, and that, when I ask for a *watercress sandwich,* I do not mean a loaf with a field in the middle of it.

Oscar Wilde

The noblest of all dogs is the *hot-dog*; it feeds the hand that bites it.

Laurence J Peter

For *rabbits* young and rabbits old,
For rabbits hot and rabbits cold,
For rabbits tender, rabbits tough,
We thank thee, Lord, we've had enough.

Grace, attributed to Jonathan Swift

Rabbit said, '*Honey* or *condensed milk* with your bread?'
(Pooh) was so excited he said, 'Both', and, so as not to seem
greedy, he added, 'But don't bother about the bread,
please.'

A A Milne, Winnie the Pooh

Out, vile *jelly!*

Shakespeare, King Lear,
III.vii

Watermelon - it is a good fruit. You eat, you drink, you
wash your face.

Enrico Caruso

A dessert without *cheese* is like a beautiful
woman with only one eye.

*Jean-Anthelme Brillat-Savarin
French gastronome
(1755-1826)*

Milk is rendered immortal in *cheese.*

Enoch Powell

I have yet room for six *scotches* more.

Shakespeare, Antony and
Cleopatra, *IV.vii*

A Nickname Is The Heaviest Stone

'A nickname is the heaviest stone that the devil can throw at a man,' wrote William Hazlitt in his essay on nicknames. Who have laboured under - or perhaps rejoiced in - the following nicknames, in fact and fiction? The answers are over the page.

1
The Butcher of Broadway

2
The Lady with the Lamp

3
America's Sweetheart/The World's Sweetheart

4
The Napoleon of Crime

5
Old Blood and Guts

6
Mr Five Per Cent

7
Superior Person

8
Phyllis and Sharon

9
Bloody Mary

10
The GOM

Answers
A Nickname Is The Heaviest Stone

1

Alexander Woolcott

2

Florence Nightingale

3

Mary Pickford

4

Professor Moriarty (in Conan Doyle's *The Final Problem*)
and Macavity the Mystery Cat (in the poem by T S Eliot)

5

General George S Patton

6

Calouste Gulbenkian, oil millionaire, whose share of the
Turkish Petroleum Co, prior to the First World War, was
reduced from 40 to 5 per cent following an Anglo-German
agreement

7

'My name is George Nathaniel Curzon,/ I am a most
superior person' - Anon, *The Masque of Balliol*

8

Rod Stewart and Elton John (their nicknames for each other)

9

Queen Mary I

10

W E Gladstone ('the Grand Old Man' - sometimes 'the
MOG', the Murderer of Gordon) or WG Grace, the cricketer

11

Queen Elizabeth I

12

Bing Crosby

13

Queen Victoria (phrase coined by Rudyard Kipling)

14

The pilots who fought in the Battle of Britain (Churchill: 'Never in the field of human conflict was so much owed by so many to so few')

15

The British Expeditionary Force, 1914 (said to stem from a remark of the Kaiser's that they were 'a contemptible little army')

16

The Home Guard in Britain, in the Second World War

17

Robespierre (coined by Carlyle in *The History of the French Revolution*)

18

P G Wodehouse or Sir Pelham Francis Warner, the cricketer

19

Turkey (Tsar Nicholas I said, in 1853: 'We have a sick man on our hands, a man gravely ill, it will be a great misfortune if one of these days he slips through our hands, especially before the necessary arrangements are made')

20

King Charles II

21

Shirley Temple, Bing Crosby or Prince Charles ('One take Wales', as Princess Anne called him, for his expertise in front of film and TV cameras)

Don't Quote Me On That

Desmond MacCarthy once said that the pressure under which journalists work necessarily makes them 'more attentive to the minute hand of history than to the hour hand'. Whatever the case, the 'fourth estate' (a phrase coined by Edmund Burke) has attracted its fair share of brickbats over the years. Here are a few of them - some of them self-inflicted:

The lowest depth to which people can sink before God is defined by the word 'journalist'. If I were a father and had a daughter who was seduced I should not despair over her; I would hope for her salvation. But if I had a son who became a journalist and continued to be one for five years, I would give him up.

Sören Kierkegaard (attrib)

If you don't know what's going on in Portugal, you must have been reading the papers.

Paul Foot, journalist, 1975

Mr Salter's side of the conversation was limited to expressions of assent. When Lord Copper was right he said, 'Definitely, Lord Copper'; when he was wrong, 'Up to a point'.

of the Foreign Editor and the proprietor of 'The Beast', in Evelyn Waugh's Scoop

News is what a chap who doesn't care much about anything wants to read.

Waugh, again

A spirit of national masochism prevails, encouraged by an effete corps of impudent snobs who characterise themselves as intellectuals.

Spiro Agnew, 1969 ('The nattering nabobs of negativism' attack referred to the broadcast media, too)

Memories don't last as long as you people in the media think.

Harold Wilson, 1975

To the born editor, news is great fun, even as the capsizing of a boat in Sydney Harbour is great fun for the sharks.

Bernard Shaw

Editor: a person employed by a newspaper whose business it is to separate the wheat from the chaff and to see that the chaff is printed.

Elbert Hubbard

Journalism consists largely in saying 'Lord Jones Died' to people who never knew Lord Jones was alive.

G K Chesterton

(Written) by office boys for office boys.

Lord Salisbury (1830-1903)
of the Daily Mail

It will be all tits, bums, QPR and roll your own fags.

attributed to Derek Jameson,
editor in chief Express
Newspapers on the launching
of the Daily Star

SMALL EARTHQUAKE IN CHILE-NOT MANY DEAD

When Claud Cockburn worked on *The Times,* someone invented a competition with a small prize to see who could write the dullest headline and actually get it printed in the paper. Cockburn only won the prize once, with the above headline.

Here are some headlines which betray a sense of fun among the sub-editors who devised them:

Equity Blacks Othello

London
Daily Telegraph

CHIP SHOP OWNER BATTERED MAN

Gateshead Post

NUT SCREWS WASHERS & BOLTS

probably apocryphal headline referring to mental patient who raped two laundry-workers and escaped

THE END OF THE WORLD

Scottish Daily Express *(not quite as bad as it sounds-the Scotland football team had been defeated in the World Cup)*

Book lack in Ongar

Private Eye, *on a librarians' strike in Essex*

INCEST MORE COMMON THAN THOUGHT IN U.S.

British newspaper

SEX CHANGE MONK ONCE A ROYAL FOOTMAN

*Yorkshire
Evening Post*

THEY'RE OFF, HAROLD TELLS QUEEN

*London
Evening Standard*

NUDIST WELFARE MAN'S MODEL WIFE FELL FOR THE CHINESE HYPNOTIST FROM THE CO-OP BACON FACTORY

News of the World

Whether the sub-editors who devised *these* headlines knew what they were doing, I'm not so sure:

COLETTE: GRAND OLD LADY OF FRENCH LETTERS

The Scotsman

MACARTHUR FLIES BACK TO FRONT

after a confrontation with President Truman in Washington

NEGLIGENCE ALLEGED OVER LOSS OF LEG

The Scotsman

ICELANDIC FISH TALKS~ NOT LIKELY

Grimsby Evening Telegraph

Eighth Army push bottles up Germans

British newspaper

Dullest Gazette

Youth hit by Train is rushed to two Hospitals

Harrow Observer

STEPS TO HELP HILL FARMERS URGED

Dundee Courier & Advertiser

ARCHAEOLOGISTS ATTACK DEAD ELEPHANT

Athens News

POPE DIES AGAIN

British newspaper, 1978

That Title From A Better Man I Stole - 2

It is hard to say with certainty where Jane Austen found the title for her novel, *Pride and Prejudice*. Perhaps it was from Gibbon's *The Decline and Fall of the Roman Empire*. Of the enfranchisement of slaves, he wrote: 'Without destroying the distinction of ranks a distant prospect of freedom and honours was presented, even to those whom pride and prejudice almost disdained to number among the human species.' More likely, Jane Austen took her cue from Fanny Burney's novel, *Cecilia*, which contains the words three times, printed in bold type: 'The whole of this unfortunate business,' said Dr Lyster, 'has been the result of *Pride and Prejudice* .. Yet this, however, remember; if to *Pride and Prejudice* you owe your miseries, so wonderfully is good and evil balanced, that to *Pride and Prejudice* you will also owe their termination.'

Where did these other novelists take their titles from? The answers are on page 52.

1
Thomas Wolfe: *Look Homeward, Angel*

2
Nicholas Meyer: *The Seven Per Cent Solution*

3
Arthur Koestler: *Scum of the Earth*

4
Mary McCarthy: *Cast a Cold Eye*

5
Robert Player: *Let's Talk of Graves, of Worms and Epitaphs*

6
Agatha Christie: *By the Pricking of my Thumbs*

7

Agatha Christie: *Sad Cypress*

8

Constantine Fitzgibbon: *When the Kissing had to Stop*

9

James Herriot: *All Creatures Great and Small*

10

Anthony Burgess: *Nothing Like the Sun*

11

Henry James: *The Golden Bowl*

12

Marcel Proust: *Remembrance of Things Past*

13

What quotation links two titles of novels by Irwin Shaw
with one of John Le Carré?

Answers
That Title From A Better Man I Stole - 2

1

Milton, *Lycidas:* 'Look homeward, Angel, now, and melt with ruth.'

2

Conan Doyle, *The Sign of Four*: (Holmes to Watson) 'It is cocaine . . . a seven per cent solution. Would you care to try it?'

3

The Duke of Wellington: '(Our army) is composed of the scum of the earth - the mere scum of the earth.'

4

W B Yeats, *Under Ben Bulben* (also his epitaph): 'Cast a cold eye/On Life, on Death/ Horseman, pass by!'

5

Shakespeare, *Richard II,* III,ii

6

Shakespeare, *Macbeth,* IV,i: 'By the pricking of my thumbs, something wicked this way comes.'

7

Shakespeare, *Twelfth Night,* II,iv: 'Come away, come away, death,/ And in sad cypress let me be laid.'

8

Browning, *A Toccata at Galuppi's*: 'What of soul was left, I wonder, when the kissing had to stop.'

9

Mrs Cecil Frances Alexander, the hymn 'All Things Bright and Beautiful'.

10

Shakespeare, *Sonnets,* 130: 'My mistress' eyes are nothing like the sun.'

11

Ecclesiastes, 12:6: 'Or ever . . . the golden bowl be broken . . . then shall the dust return to the earth as it was.'

12

Shakespeare, *Sonnets,* 30: 'When to the sessions of sweet silent thought/ I summon up remembrance of things past.'

13

John Le Carré, *Tinker, Tailor, Solder, Spy*; Irwin Shaw, *Rich Man, Poor Man*; Irwin Shaw, *Beggar Man, Thief* - all based on the children's rhyme, 'Tinker, Tailor, Soldier, Sailor'.

Playing Piano In A Whorehouse

'Movie script-writing is no worse than playing piano in a whorehouse,' asserted S J Perelman on one occasion. Never mind the whores - in which pictures would you come across the following pearls from the scriptwriters' typewriters? The answers are on page 58.

1

May the force be with you!

2

You're going out a youngster, but you've got to come back a star

3

Frankly, my dear, I don't give a damn

4

To boldly go where no man has gone before

5

The world shall hear from me again

6

Of all the gin joints in all the towns in all the world, she walks into mine

7

What he did to Shakespeare, we are doing now to Poland

8

Is this the end of Rico?

9

I *cannot* live without my life . . . I *cannot* love without my soul

---

10

Your idea of fidelity is not going to bed with more than one man at a time

11

Out of the cradle, endlessly rocking

12

Either he's dead, or my watch has stopped

Answers
Playing Piano In A Whorehouse

1
Star Wars

2
Forty-Second Street - Warner Baxter as the producer to Ruby Keeler as the chorus-girl who has to take over from the star

3
Gone With the Wind - Clark Gable as 'Rhett Butler' to Vivien Leigh as 'Scarlett O'Hara'

4
Star Trek
(the TV series)

5
The Face of Fu Manchu (etc)

6
Casablanca

7
To Be or not To Be - Gestapo chief, of actor (played by Jack Benny)

8
Little Caesar - Edward G. Robinson, expiring

9
Wuthering Heights - Laurence Olivier as 'Heathcliff' (1939) - a direct quote from Emily Brontë's novel

10
Darling - Dirk Bogarde of Julie Christie

11

Intolerance - much-repeated caption

12

A Night at the Opera - the Marx Brothers

Messages Are For Western Union

Both Sam Goldwyn and Harry Warner are credited with the above terse rejection of films with a moral or social message. On the other hand, here are some occasions when the messages were indeed for Western Union - or the British Post Office:

G K Chesterton once wired his wife:

AM IN WOLVERHAMPTON. WHERE OUGHT I TO BE?

Dorothy Parker sent a telegram to Mrs Robert Sherwood, who had made heavy weather of her pregnancy and had at last given birth:

DEAR MARY WE KNEW YOU HAD IT IN YOU.

On another occasion, Dorothy Parker wired two friends who had been living together and then got married:

WHAT'S NEW?

Noel Coward was an inveterate sender of telegrams. To his companion, Cole Lesley, he wired:

AM BACK FROM ISTANBUL WHERE I WAS KNOWN AS ENGLISH DELIGHT.

When he was staying in Florence, he cabled home:

HAVE MOVED HOTEL EXCELSIOR. COUGHING MYSELF INTO A FIRENZE

Having agreed to see a production of one of his plays at Bury St Edmunds, he was also invited to attend a service commemorating the saint who gave his name to the town. He declined thus:

I COME TO BURY ST EDMUNDS NOT TO PRAISE HIM

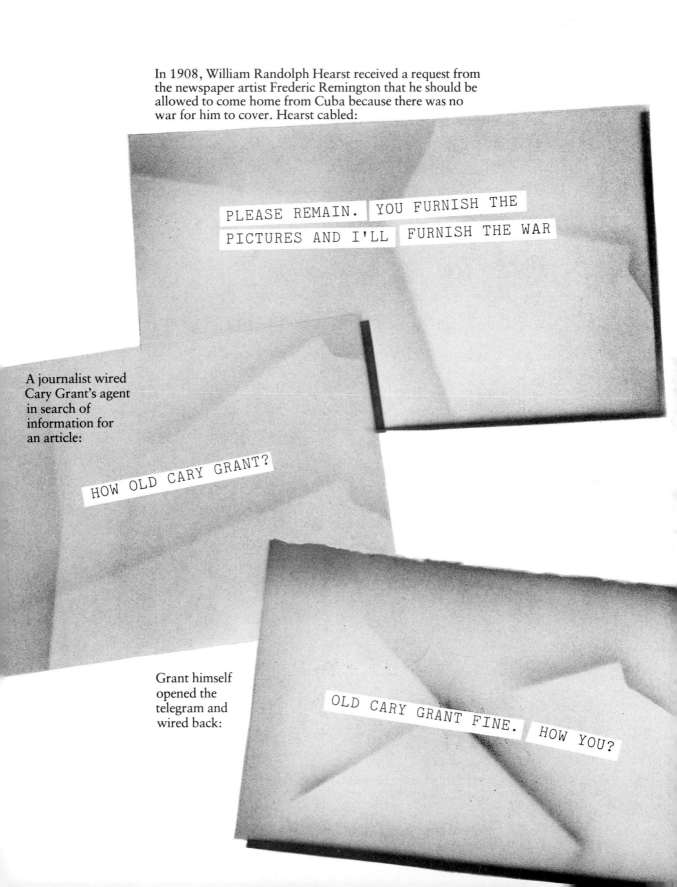

In 1908, William Randolph Hearst received a request from the newspaper artist Frederic Remington that he should be allowed to come home from Cuba because there was no war for him to cover. Hearst cabled:

PLEASE REMAIN. YOU FURNISH THE PICTURES AND I'LL FURNISH THE WAR

A journalist wired Cary Grant's agent in search of information for an article:

HOW OLD CARY GRANT?

Grant himself opened the telegram and wired back:

OLD CARY GRANT FINE. HOW YOU?

When the Associated Press mistakenly announced Mark Twain's death, the author, who was on a visit to Europe, wired New York:

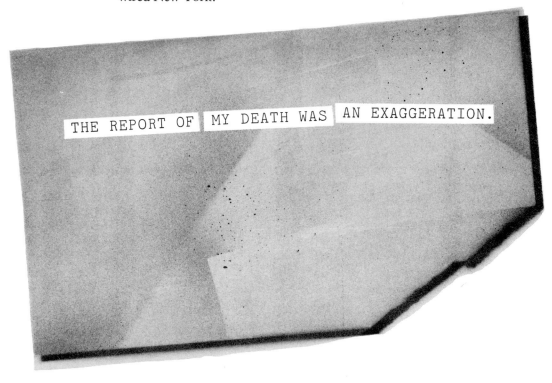

THE REPORT OF MY DEATH WAS AN EXAGGERATION.

Anonymous sports journalist:

HOPEFULLY HERE AT OLYMPICS TO WIN 100 LITRES

When Dorothy Parker repaid a loan to John Gilbert he sent
her this telegram:

THANK YOU MISS FINLAND

(Finland was the only nation to repay its First World War
debts to the United States)

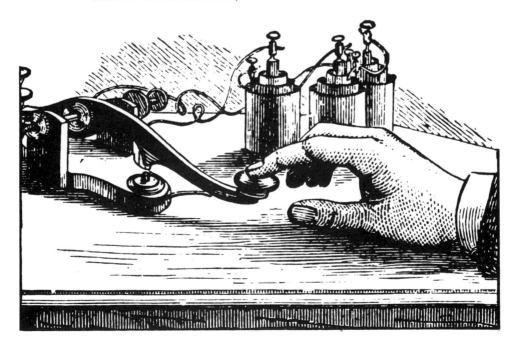

I Went To Philadelphia, But It Was Closed

There was no love lost between W C Fields and the City of Brotherly Love, as the above quotation (among others) makes clear. The remark has also been applied to other places which do not encourage a complimentary postcard home. Where were these people talking about? The answers are over the page.

1

There is no city in the US in which I get a warmer welcome and fewer votes than _____

John F Kennedy

2

I look upon _____ as an inferior sort of Scotland

Revd Sydney Smith

3

I saw a notice which said 'Drink _____ Dry' and I've just started

Brendan Behan

4

I have lived 78 years without hearing of bloody places like _____

Winston Churchill, 1953

5

Worth seeing but not worth going to see

Samuel Johnson

6

_____ was long a despotism tempered by epigrams

Thomas Carlyle

7

I was the toast of two continents: _____ and _____

Dorothy Parker

8

_____ is all suburb and no urb.

Alan Coren

9

Before this time tomorrow I shall have gained a peerage or _____

Horatio Nelson

10

_____ is at the present moment the centre of the consciousness of the human universe.

Allen Ginsberg, circa 1964

11

_____ is on the whole more attractive than _____ to the ordinary visitor; and the traveller is therefore recommended to visit _____ first, or to omit it altogether if he cannot visit both.

Baedeker's Great Britain (1887): 'From London to Oxford'

12

To the glory that was _____
And the grandeur that was _____

Edgar Allan Poe, To Helen

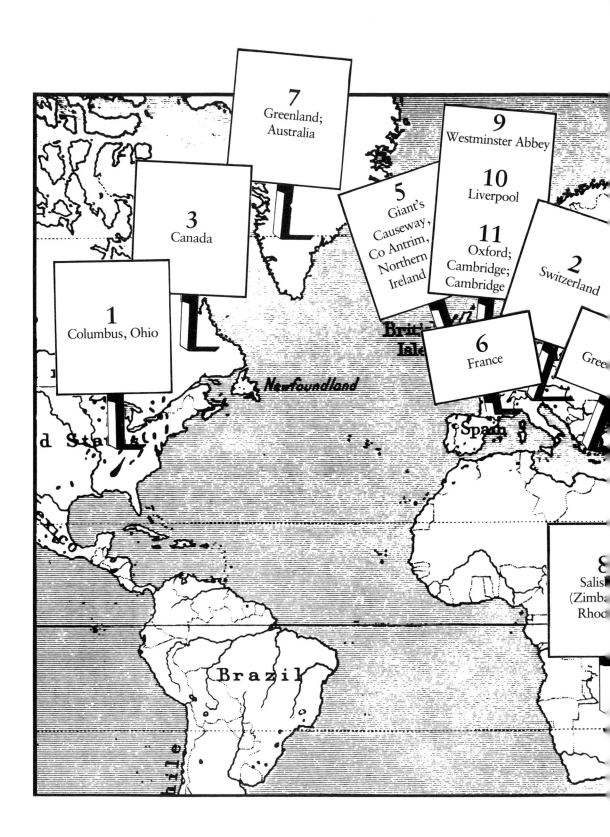

7 Greenland; Australia

9 Westminster Abbey

3 Canada

5 Giant's Causeway, Co Antrim, Northern Ireland

10 Liverpool

2 Switzerland

1 Columbus, Ohio

11 Oxford; Cambridge; Cambridge

6 France

Gree

Newfoundland

Brit Isle

Spain

8 Salis (Zimba Rhod

Brazil

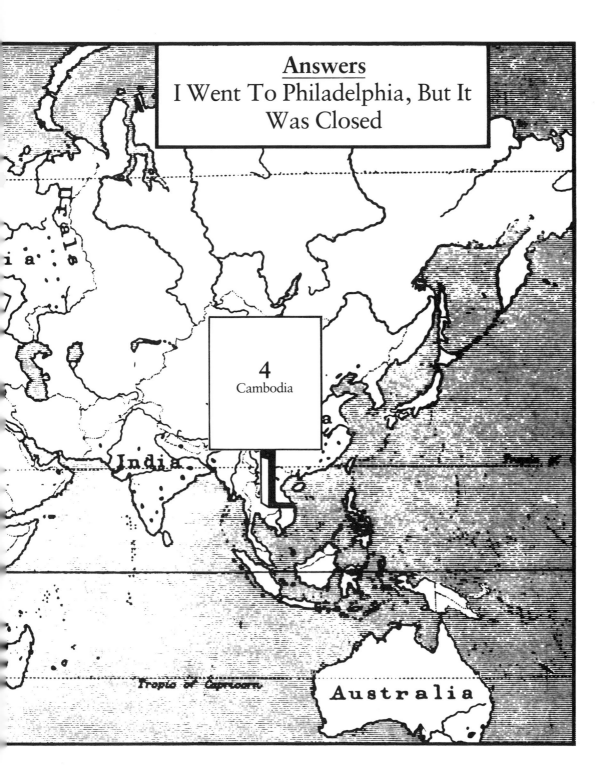

Answers
I Went To Philadelphia, But It
Was Closed

4
Cambodia

Sic Biscuitus Disintegrat*

There are some quotations about which comment would be superfluous. I'll let these speak for themselves:

Capitalism is the exploitation of man by man. Communism is the exact reverse.

Anon

Ah, what is man? Wherefore does he why? Whence did he whence? Whither is he withering?

Dan Leno, music-hall star

I tell you, cocaine isn't habit-forming. I know, because I've been taking it for years.

Tallulah Bankhead

Life is like a sewer - what you take out depends on what you put into it.

Tom Lehrer

Remember that you are an Englishman and have consequently won first prize in the lottery of life.

Cecil Rhodes

There are only three men who have ever understood it (the Schleswig-Holstein question). One was Prince Albert, who is dead. The second was a German professor, who became mad. I am the third and I have forgotten all about it.

Viscount Palmerston, 1863

I have made my contribution to society. I have no plans to work again.

John Lennon, 1977

Well, you see, he doesn't bark and he knows the secrets of the sea.

Gérard de Nerval, French Poet (1808-55), when asked why he took a pet lobster through the streets of Paris on a long blue leash

---

* That's the way the cookie crumbles

This was the first occasion for several years that Scott and
Thorpe had met face to face.

> *BBC reporter, on first*
> *appearance of Norman Scott at*
> *the Minehead magistrates'*
> *hearing of the Jeremy Thorpe*
> *case, 1978*

A fat man should not play the concertina.

> *Mao Tse-Tung*

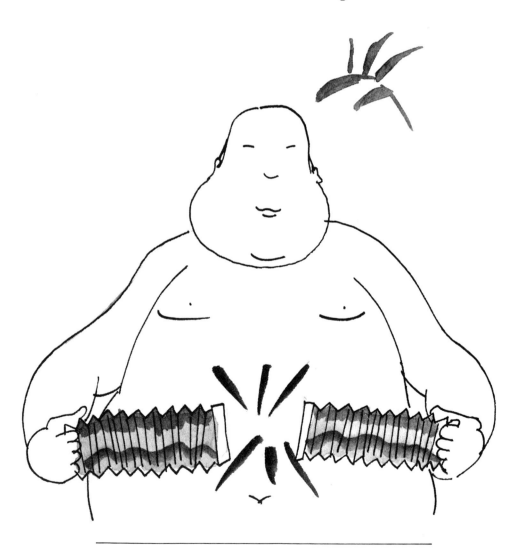

I don't know who's ahead. It's either Oxford or Cambridge

> *John Snagge, commentary on*
> *Oxford and Cambridge*
> *University Boat Race, 1949*

He spent his declining years trying to guess the answer to the Irish question. Unfortunately whenever he was getting warm, the Irish secretly changed the question.

> *Sellar and Yeatman,* 1066 and
> All That

I know I am God because when I pray to him I find I'm talking to myself

> *Fourteenth Earl of Gurney, in*
> The Ruling Class *by Peter*
> *Barnes*

Your experience will be a lesson to all of us men to be careful not to marry ladies in very high positions.

> *Idi Amin to Lord Snowdon, on*
> *his divorce*

I never knew the lower classes had such white skins.

> *First Marquess Curzon of*
> *Kedleston*

I would walk over my grandmother if necessary to get Nixon re-elected

> *Charles W. Colson, when*
> *Special Counsel to the*
> *President. Now, a born-again*
> *Christian, he walks on the*
> *water instead*

I'm interested in stories about people as we knew them in the near-recent future.

> *Philip Kaufman,* Star Trek
> *writer/director*

It is difficult to love mankind unless one has a reasonable private income. And if one has a reasonable private income one has better things to do than love mankind.

Hugh Kingsmill

As God once said - and I think rightly . . .

Field Marshal Lord Montgomery

Q. Are you Jewish?
A. No, a tree fell on me.

Spike Milligan

If I were a man, I would be Richard Burton. But as I am a woman, I will be Richard Burton's wife.

Lady Burton, wife of the nineteenth-century explorer

The situation in Zimbabwe is a war situation

Robert Mugabe, 1978

It popped on its little drawers

Revd W A Spooner

It is no further from the north coast of Spitzbergen to the North Pole than it is from Land's End to John of Gaunt

Spooner again

Poor soul, very sad. Her late husband, you know - a very sad death - eaten by missionaries.

Spooner again

The Lord is a shoving leopard

Spooner again

Reporter: What do you think of Western Civilisation?
Mahatma Gandhi: I think it would be a very good idea

The art of the quill has been practised since Caxton - and probably before

David Frost, in radio interview with the author, 1977

An archaeologist is the best husband any woman can have; the older she gets, the more interested he is in her.

attributed to Agatha Christie (who was married to the archaeologist Sir Max Mallowan), but authorship firmly denied by her

Bishop: My palace has forty bedrooms in it.
Winston Churchill: And only Thirty-Nine Articles to put in them.

Field officers must not wear spurs when taking passage in captive balloons.

King's Regulations, early nineteenth century

I'm a one-eyed Jewish negro

*Sammy Davis Jnr, when asked
what his golf handicap was*

Well, he seemed such a nice old gentleman, I thought I would
give him my autograph as a souvenir.

*attributed to Adolf Hitler,
about Neville Chamberlain
and the Munich Agreement,
1938*

If the court sentences the blighter to hang, then the blighter
will hang.

*General Zia of Pakistan about
former Prime Minister Bhutto,
executed 1979*

When one subtracts from life infancy (which is vegetation),
sleep, eating, and swilling - buttoning and unbuttoning
-how much remains of downright existence? - the summer
of a dormouse.

Byron, Diary, *December
1813*

Television is for appearing on, not looking at.

Noel Coward

Wife beating may be socially acceptable in Sheffield but it is
a different matter in Cheltenham.

Lord Justice Lawton

It was easy after the first one. After that I was trying for the
Guinness Book of Records.

*Archibald Hall, 'the gay
butler', convicted of five
murders, 1978*

We in the industry know that behind every successful
screenwriter stands a woman. And behind her stands his
wife.

Groucho Marx

There are three things I always forget: names, faces and . . .
I can't remember the other.

Italo Svevo

How dare they describe this thing I've worked at in my
voicebox as shouting? I always feel my voice is like black
velvet on sandpaper.

Rod Stewart

I always wait for *The Times* each morning. I look at the
obituary column, and if I'm not in it, I go to work.

*A E Matthews, actor, whose
obituary appeared in* The
Times *on 26 July 1960*

The Great Wall, I've been told, is the only man-made
structure on earth that is visible from the moon. For the life
of me I cannot see why anyone would go to the moon to
look at it, when, with almost the same difficulty, it can be
viewed in China.

J K Galbraith

Quand je regarde mon derrière, je vois qu'il est divisé en
deux parties.

*Winston Churchill, looking
back over his past, in a
speech in Paris*

A man may surely be allowed to take a glass of wine by his
own fireside.

*Richard Sheridan, taking
refreshment at the Piazza
Coffee House in Covent
Garden while the Drury Lane
Theatre, which he owned,
was burning down, 1809*

Woman: I think you're terribly outspoken.
Dorothy Parker: Outspoken by whom?

I am fond of children (except boys).

Lewis Carroll

I love children - especially when they cry, for then someone takes them away.

Nancy Mitford

Gambler: Is this a game of chance?
W C Fields: Not the way I play it.

My Little Chickadee

It's all part of life's rich pageant.

Peter Sellers as Inspector Clouseau, having just opened his car door and fallen into a pond

Anybody seen in a bus after the age of thirty has been a failure in life.

Loelia, Duchess of Westminster

An alcoholic is someone you don't like who drinks as much as you do.

Dylan Thomas

Everything's at sea - except the Fleet.

Horace Walpole

The army works like this: if a man dies when you hang him, keep hanging him until he gets used to it.

Spike Milligan

There can hardly be a town in the south of England where you could throw a brick without hitting the niece of a Bishop.

George Orwell

We have become, Nina, the sort of people our parents warned us about.

Augustus John to Nina Hamnett

Friends are God's apology for relations.

Hugh Kingsmill

It was three o'clock in the morning in New York. It was
pouring with rain, and it came to me . . . 'And now the end
is near and so I face the final curtain' . . . And I said wow
that's it, that's for Sinatra . . . and then I cried.

*Paul Anka, on completing the
lyrics of 'My Way'*

*A Yorkshire miner put in a very late claim for
compensation.*
Judge to Counsel: Your client is no doubt aware of
vigilantibus, et non dormientibus, jura subveniunt?
Counsel: In Barnsley, m'lud, they speak of little else.

If there's one thing above all a vulture can't stand, it's a
glass eye.

Frank McKinney Hubbard

Quoth . . . Misquoth

Could anything worse have been said of William Prynne (1600-69), the Puritan pamphleteer, than this: 'He was a learned man, of immense reading, but is much blamed for his unfaithful quotations'?

On the other hand, Hesketh Pearson once wrote that 'misquotation is the pride and privilege of the learned'. So perhaps we should not be too picky in this matter.

Here are some sayings of the kind that, once heard, are never remembered accurately. What are their correct original forms? The answers are on page 84.

1

Water, water, everywhere and not a drop to drink

2

Tomorrow to fresh fields and pastures new.

3

The lion shall lie down with the lamb.

4

The cup that cheers.

5

Rule, Britannia,
Britannia rules the waves;
Britons never, never, never
Shall be slaves.

6

They shall not grow old as we that are left grow old.

7

I must warn you that anything you say may be taken down and used in evidence against you.

8

Vengeance is mine, saith the Lord.

9
Home is the sailor
Home from the sea.

83

Answers
Quoth . . . Misquoth

1

'Water, water, everywhere,/ And all the boards did shrink;/ Water, water, everywhere/ Nor any drop to drink' - Samuel Taylor Coleridge, *The Ancient Mariner*

2

'Tomorrow to fresh woods and pastures new' - Milton, *Lycidas*

3

'The wolf also shall dwell with the lamb, and the leopard shall lie down with the kid; and the calf and the young lion and the fatling together' - Isaiah 17:6

4

'The cups that cheer/ But not inebriate' - William Cowper, *The Task*

5

'Rule, Britannia,/ Britannia rule the waves;/ Britons never, never, never/ Will be slaves' - James Thomson

6

'They shall grow not old as we that are left grow old' -Laurence Binyon, *Poems for the Fallen*

7

There are various forms of the police 'caution' but none of them includes the phrase 'used in evidence against you'. A likely version is: 'You are not obliged to say anything unless you wish to do so, but what you say may be put in writing and given in evidence.'

8

'Vengeance is mine; I will repay, saith the Lord' - Romans 12:19 (which completely changes the meaning)

9

'Home is the sailor/ Home from sea' - R L Stevenson, *Requiem*

Honey, Your Silk Stocking's Hanging Down

This was the somewhat fanciful translation by Sellar and Yeatman in *1066 and All That* of the motto of the Most Noble Order of the Garter - *'Honi Soit Qui Mal y Pense'* ('Evil be to him who evil thinks'). If necessary, supply your own translations of the following mottoes of institutions and slogans from politics and advertising. More important, to whom do they / did they belong. The answers are on page 88.

1
I shall return.

2
All the news that's fit to print.

3
A land fit for heroes.

4
Ich dien.

5
Be prepared.

6
We really move our tails for you.

7
Sic semper tyrannis.

8
Eureka!

9
We ourselves.

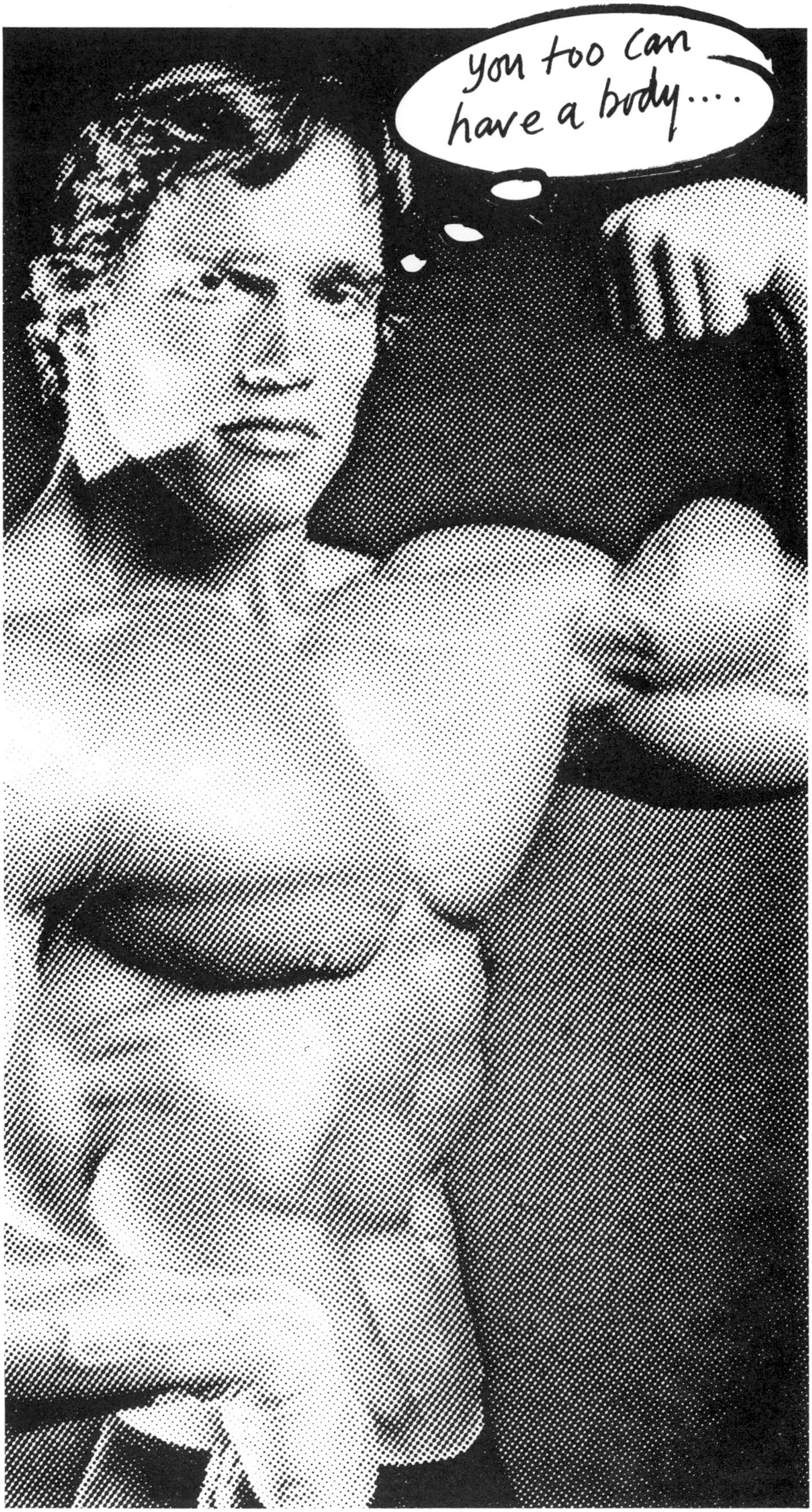
you too can
have a body....

10

You too can have a body like mine.

11

Only connect.

12

All for one, and one for all.

13

Peace in our time.

14

Why not the best?

15

Ars gratia artis.

16

Per ardua ad astra.

17

You press the button and we'll do the rest.

18

In your heart you know he's right.

Answers
Honey, Your Silk Stocking's Hanging Down

1

General Douglas MacArthur, on being forced to pull out of
the Philippines in the Second World War

2

The motto of the *New York Times,* devised by
Adolph S Ochs

3

David Lloyd George, 1918: 'What is our task? To make
Britain a fit country for heroes to live in.'

4

The motto of the Prince of Wales (German 'I serve' or
Welsh 'eich dyn' - 'your man')

5

The motto of the Boy Scout movement, based on the initials
(B-P) of its founder, Sir Robert Baden-Powell

6

Advertising slogan for Continental Airlines, which led to
the company being sued by some of its stewardesses, 1975

7

The motto of the State of Virginia - apart from being what
John Wilkes Booth cried after shooting Abraham Lincoln

8

The motto of the State of California

9

The motto of - and the meaning of - Sinn Fein, the Irish
nationalist movement

10
Advertising slogan for Charles Atlas body-building courses

11
The motto of *Howard's End* by E M Forster - in fact, a quotation from the novel: 'Only connect the prose and the passion, and both will be exalted, and human love will be seen at its height.'

12
The motto of The Three Musketeers in the novel by Alexandre Dumas ('Tous pour un, un pour tous')

13
What Neville Chamberlain actually said on his return from signing the Munich agreement with Hitler in 1938 was: 'I believe it is peace *for* our time . . . peace with honour.'

14
Campaign slogan of Jimmy Carter, 1976

15
The motto of Metro-Goldwyn-Mayer, meaning 'Art for Art's sake'.

16
The motto of the Royal Air Force ('Through hardship to the stars')

17
Advertising slogan for Kodak, *circa* 1888

18
Barry Goldwater's slogan when standing against Lyndon Johnson, 1964 Presidential Election

Go Not Empty Unto Thy Mother In Law
Ruth 3:17

'The total absence of humour from the Bible is one of the most singular things in all literature', remarked Alfred North Whitehead, the philosopher. Nevertheless, a good deal of unintentional humour can be found in both Old and New Testaments. Bearing in mind G K Chesterton's dictum that 'it is the test of a good religion whether you can joke about it', let us now meditate on the followings texts (all taken from the Authorised Version, except where stated):

And he said unto her, Give me, I pray three, a little water to drink; for I am thirsty. And she opened a bottle of milk.

Judges 4:19

So we boiled my son, and did eat him.

2 Kings 6:29

For only Og king of Bashan remained of the remnant of giants; behold, his bedstead was a bedstead of iron.

Deuteronomy 3:11

He got in underneath the Elephant and thrust at it from below and killed it. It fell to the ground on top of him, and there he died.

1 Maccabees 6:46
(Apocrypha)

And all the people sat in the street trembling because of this matter, and for the great rain.

Ezra 10:9

And the lot fell upon Matthias.

Acts 1:26

And he spake to his sons, saying, Saddle me the ass. And they saddled him.

1 Kings 13:27

Even a child is known by his doings.

Proverbs 20:11

He delighteth not in the strength of the horse: he taketh not pleasure in the legs of a man.

Psalm 146:10

And Isaiah said, Take a lump of figs. And they laid it on the boil, and he recovered.

2 Kings 20:7

And Adonibezak said, Three-score and ten kings, having their thumbs and their great toes cut off, gathered their meat under my table.

Judges 1:7

He saith among the trumpets, Ha, Ha.

Job 39:25

And I will take away mind hand, and thou shalt see my back parts.

Exodus 33:23

As she sat on the ass, she broke wind, and Caleb said, 'What did you mean by that?' She replied, 'I want to ask a favour of you.'

Judges 1:14 (New English Bible)

How Different From The Home Life Of Our Own Dear Queen

The story has it that, during a performance of *Antony and Cleopatra* - perhaps with Sarah Bernhardt in the lead - in which the actress ranted and raved around the stage, pulling down the scenery, one Victorian matron turned to another and remarked: 'How different, how very different from the home life of our own dear Queen.'

By or about which Royals (not all of them British) were the following remarks made? The answers are on page 96.

1

Well, Mr Baldwin, *this* is a pretty kettle of fish.

2

It's nice to know I can do something right for a change.

3

The one advantage about marrying a princess - or someone from a royal family - is that they do know what happens.

4

Let me introduce you to my widow.

5

The King's life is moving peacefully towards its close.

6

I don't mind 'im 'avin 'er for 'is goin's on - but as Queen of England - *that* I will *not* 'ave.

7

One was presented with a small hairy individual and, out of general curiosity, one climbed on.

8

A lady whom we respect because she is our Queen and whom we love because she is herself.

9

We are all socialists now.

10

It is one of the incidents of the profession.

11

I think it is about time we pulled our finger out.

12

I never see any home cooking. All I get is fancy stuff.

13

I ask you to commend him to God's Grace which he will so
abundantly need . . . if he is to do this duty faithfully. We
hope that he is aware of his need. Some of us wish that he
gave more positive signs of his awareness.

14

If — ever sets foot in Chicago, I'll punch him in the snoot.

15

I have fallen in love with all sorts of girls and I fully intend
to go on doing so.

16

Things were done better in my day.

17

Only two rules really count: never miss an opportunity to
relieve yourself; never miss a chance to sit down and rest
your feet.

18

I think on this occasion I may be forgiven for saying, 'My
husband and I . . .'

Answers

How Different From The Home Life Of Our Own Dear Queen

1

Queen Mary to Stanley Baldwin on Edward VIII's liaison with Mrs Wallis Simpson.

2

Captain Mark Phillips, when it was announced that Princess Anne was pregnant, 1977

3

Prince Charles

4

King Leopold II of Belgium (d 1909). On learning that he must undergo a serious operation (which did indeed prove fatal) he sent for his No. 1 mistress (a twenty-five year old ex-prostitute whom he had made a Baroness) and married her. When the ceremony was over, he said this to his Best Man, the Prime Minister.

5

King George V. On the evening of 20 January 1936 the BBC cancelled all programmes. Every fifteen minutes the terms of the medical bulletin were read out including this phrase until the news of the King's death was announced.

6

Cockney char about Edward VIII

7

Princess Anne, on her first encounter with a horse

8
Winston Churchill on Elizabeth II, Coronation Day
broadcast, 1953

9
Edward VII, 1895

10
Umberto I of Italy, talking about an attempt on his life. He
was eventually assassinated in 1900

11
Prince Philip, 1961

12
Ditto

13
Alfred Blunt, Bishop of Bradford, whose address to a
diocesan conference on 1 December 1936, about Edward
VIII, unwittingly provided the British press with an
opportunity to break its silence on the Abdication crisis
(although this was not what the Bishop was talking about).

14
William Hale Thompson, Mayor of Chicago, on George V,
during a period of anti-British feeling

15
Prince Charles

16
Mrs Alice Keppel, mistress of Edward VII, on the day of
Edward VIII's Abdication

17
Edward VIII, as Duke of Windsor

18
Elizabeth II, at Silver Wedding banquet, 1972

The Buck Stops Here

'When I was a boy,' said Clarence Darrow, 'I was told that anybody could become President of the United States; I'm beginning to believe it.' The following sayings are all from men who did make it to the White House. Who were they? The answers are on page 100.

1
The son of a bitch isn't going to resign on me, I want him fired.

2
I shall not seek and I will not accept the nomination of my party for another term as your President.

3
The business of America is business.

4
I do not think it entirely inappropriate to introduce myself to this audience. I am the man who accompanied — to Paris.

5
I've got his pecker in my pocket.

6
The only thing we have to fear is fear itself.

7
My fellow citizens, the President is dead, but the government lives and God omnipotent reigns.

8
You fellows, in your business, you have a way of handling problems like this. Somebody leaves a pistol in the drawer. I don't have a pistol.

9

We must guard against the acquisition of unwarranted
influence, whether sought or unsought, by the military-
industrial complex.

10

If you are as happy, my dear sir, on entering this house (the
White House) as I am in leaving it and returning home, you
are the happiest man in the country.

11

He mobilised the English language and sent it into battle.

12

I desire the Poles carnally.

Answers
The Buck Stops Here

1
Harry S Truman (of General Douglas MacArthur)

2
Lyndon B Johnson, 1968

3
Calvin Coolidge

4
John F Kennedy (of Jackie Kennedy) during a visit to Paris, 1961.

5
Lyndon B Johnson (when Senate Majority leader)

6
Franklin D Roosevelt, 1933

7
James A. Garfield (when still a Congressman) of Lincoln's assassination.

8
Richard M Nixon (to General Alexander Haig, 7 August 1974)

9
Dwight D. Eisenhower, farewell message, 1961

10
James Buchanan (to Abraham Lincoln, the day of his retirement, 1861).

11
John F Kennedy (conferring honorary US citizenship on Winston Churchill, 1963, using words first spoken by Ed Murrow, 1954).

12
Jimmy Carter (as translated by an inadequate interpreter on a visit to Poland, 1978)

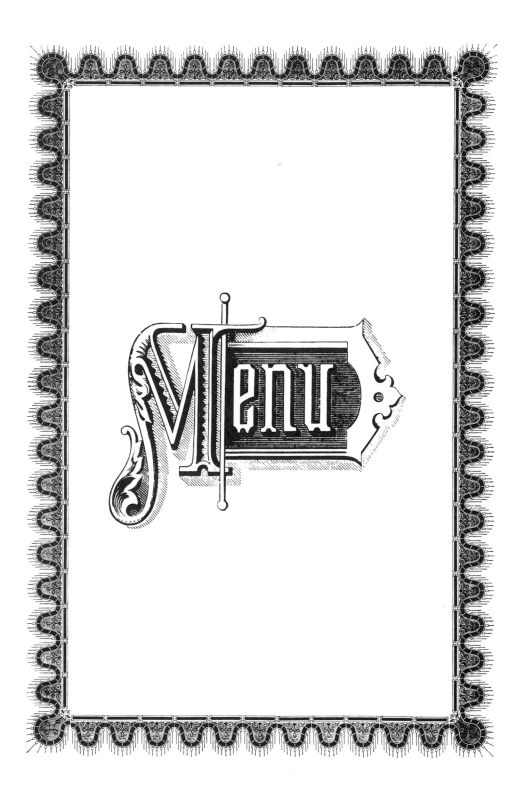

" Quote . . . Table d'Hôte "

When a new restaurant opened near Bromley in Kent, a critic wrote: 'Geographically, it is halfway between Elmer's End and Pratt's Bottom. Gastronomically, it is about the same.' The following menu does not come from that restaurant (though it sounds as though it might). It is made up of misprints and mistranslations observed on actual menus in restaurants as far apart as Ely, Athens, Venice, Funchal, Paris, Torremolinos, and in Japan, Kenya, Jamaica, Crete, Libya, and the United States.

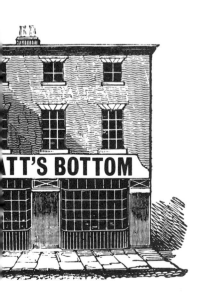

COCKTAILS

All cocktails are served with a cherry and a small
wooden prick.

STARTERS

Potage of Soup
Shrotted Pimps
Shrimps in Spit
Roll Map
Foul Soup
Gratinated Nuddles

FISH COURSE

Sole Bonne Femme (Fish Landlady Style)
Sweating Lobster
Boiled Frogfish
Drowned Squid

MAIN COURSE

Porn Shops
Veal in Breadcrumbs Friend in Butter
Bacon and Germs
Yellow Lasagne - Tuesday
Green Lasagne - Wednesday
Tasteful Chicken in Paperbag
Potatoes in Shirt
English Teak and Kidney

SWEETS

Assiette Anglaise (Dishy Englishwoman)
Jam Trat
La Spume du Chef (with Ice)
Sherry Trifle and Randy Snaps
Sweat from the Trolley

Garlic Coffee

For bad service - ask for the manager.

That Title From A Better Man I
Stole - 3

The film *A Man for All Seasons* (based on Robert Bolt's play) took its title from a saying of a contemporary of Sir Thomas More, Robert Whittington: '(He is) a man of marvellous mirth and pastimes; and sometimes of as sad gravity - a man for all seasons.' This echoes a comment on More by Erasmus. From which, rather less obscure, sources did these films take their titles - apart, that is, from any books they may have been based on?

The answers are on page 106.

1
Quo Vadis?

2
Is Paris Burning?

3
Sabrina Fair

4
A Time to Love and a Time to Die

5
A Bridge Too Far

6
What's Up, Doc?

7
Chimes at Midnight

8
I accuse

9
Such Men are Dangerous

10
Straight on till Morning

Where did the writers of these autobiographies take their titles from?

11
Evelyn Waugh: *A Little Learning*

12
King Hussein of Jordan: *Uneasy Lies the Head*

13
Rosemary Clooney: *This for Remembrance*

14
Beverley Nichols: *The Unforgiving Minute*

15
Malcolm Muggeridge: *Chronicles of Wasted Time*

16
Frederic Warburg: *All Authors are Equal*

17
Lady Diana Cooper: *The Rainbow Comes and Goes; The Light of Common Day;* and *Trumpets from the Steep.*

18
Edward G Robinson: *All My Yesterdays*

Answers
That Title From A Better Man I Stole - 3

1
St John 16:5 (Vulgate) and the Apocryphal *Acts of Peter*:
'Whither goest thou?'

2
Attributed to Hitler, 25 August 1944, the day of the
liberation of Paris (in German, 'Brennt Paris?')

3
Milton, *Comus*

4
Ecclesiastes 3:1: 'To everything there is a season, and a time
to every purpose under the heaven: A time to be born, and a
time to die . . . a time to love, and a time to hate'

5
Lieutenant General Sir Frederick Browning's protest to Field
Marshal Montgomery about the airborne landings in the
Netherlands (1944) to capture eleven bridges needed for the
invasion of Germany - 'But, sir, we may be going a bridge too far'

6
The catchphrase of Bugs Bunny

7
Shakespeare, *King Henry IV, Part II,* III,ii: 'We have heard
the chimes at midnight, Master Shallow'

8
'J'accuse' - the title of Émile Zola's open letter to the French
Government about the Dreyfus affair

9
Shakespeare, *Julius Caesar,* I.ii: 'Yond' Cassius has a lean
and hungry look;/ He thinks too much: such men are dangerous'

10

J M Barrie, *Peter Pan and Wendy*: 'Second to the right, and straight on till morning'

11

Pope, *An Essay on Criticism:* 'A little learning is a dang'rous thing'

12

Shakespeare, *King Henry IV, Part II,* III,i: 'Uneasy lies the head that wears a crown'

13

Shakespeare, *Hamlet,* IV,v: 'There's Rosemary, that's for remembrance'

14

Rudyard Kipling, *If:* 'If you can fill the unforgiving minute / With sixty seconds' worth of distance run'

15

Shakespeare, *Sonnets,* 106: 'When in the chronicles of wasted time / I see descriptions of the fairest wights'

16

George Orwell, *Animal Farm*: 'All animals are equal, but some animals are more equal than others.' Warburg published the book after several other firms had turned it down.

17

Wordsworth, *Ode (Intimations of Immortality)*: 'The Rainbow comes and goes, / And lovely is the Rose'; / 'At length the Man perceives it die away, / And fade into the light of common day'; 'The Cataracts blow their trumpets from the steep, / No more shall grief of mine the season wrong.'

18

Shakespeare, *Macbeth,* V,v: 'And all our yesterdays have lighted fools / The way to dusty death.'

Four Legs Good, Two Legs Bad

George Orwell's slogan from *Animal Farm* had nothing to do with sex - or with what Shakespeare described as 'the beast with two backs'. However, it seems an apt description for the quotations below - first, those about marital pleasures; second, about extramarital pleasures; and third, about various deviations from the norm (some actually requiring unusual combinations of more than two legs):

Marriage - the longing for the deep, deep peace of the double-bed after the hurly-burly of the chaise longue.

> *Mrs Patrick Campbell*

It is not the wild, ecstatic leap across that I deplore. It is the weary trudge home.

> *Anon,* Double Beds versus Single Beds

The only really happy people are married women and single men.

> *H L Mencken*

He has the body of a twenty-five-year-old. *

> *Margaret Trudeau, of her husband, Pierre*

Marriage is popular because it combines the maximum of temptation with the maximum of opportunity.

> *Bernard Shaw*

His Grace returned from the wars today and pleasured me twice in his top-boots.

> *Sarah Duchess of Marlborough*

---

*And he keeps it in the fridge. *Spike Milligan*

A Little Bit On The Side

A mistress should be like a little country retreat near the town; not to dwell in constantly, but only for a night and away!

> The Country Wife, I.1,
> *William Wycherley*

For my part I keep the commandments, I love my neighbour as myselfe, and to avoid Coveting my neighbour's wife I desire to be coveted by her; which you know is quite another thing.

> *William Congreve, on himself, 1700*

I can't take dictation. I can't type. I can't even answer the phone.

> *Elizabeth Ray, the Washington 'secretary' of Congressman Wayne Hays, 1976*

Various Pleasures, Horizontal and Otherwise

It doesn't matter what you do in the bedroom as long as you don't do it in the street and frighten the horses.

> *Mrs Patrick Campbell*

Hooray, hooray
The first day of May
Outdoor sex
Begins today.

> *Old rhyme*

He was into animal husbandry - until they caught him at it.

> *Tom Lehrer*

There are nine and sixty ways of constructing tribal lays
And every single one of them is right.

> *Rudyard Kipling,* In the Neolithic Age

Henry's idea of sex is to slow down to thirty miles an hour
when he drops you off at the door.

> *Barbara Howar, of Henry*
> *Kissinger*

Sex between a man and a woman can be wonderful
-provided you get between the right man and the right woman.

> *Woody Allen*

Liza: Wot's it feel like, bein' in love, Kytie?
Katie: Ow, it's prime, Liza. It's like 'avin 'ot treacle runnin'
daown yer back.

> *caption to late Victorian*
> *cartoon in* Punch *drawn by*
> *Sir Bernard Partridge*

Certain women should be struck regularly like gongs.

> Private Lives, Act III,
> *Noel Coward*

Many years ago I chased a woman for almost two years,
only to discover her tastes were exactly like mine: we were
both crazy about girls.

> *Groucho Marx*

I belong to the fag-end of Victorian liberalism.

> *E M Forster, broadcast talk, 1946*

If God had meant to have homosexuals, he'd have created
Adam and Bruce.

> *Anita Bryant, Florida, 1977*

Buggery is now almost grown as common among our
gallants as in Italy, and . . . the very pages of the town begin
to complain of their masters for it. But blessed be God, I do
not to this day know what is the meaning of this sin, nor
which is the agent nor which the patient.

> *Samuel Pepys,* Diary, *1 July 1663*

Because he spills his seed on the ground.

> *Dorothy Parker, when asked*
> *why she called her canary Onan.*

66 And Yours I See Is Coming Down 99

This most curious 'next-to-last word' in literature comes from *The Cenci* by Shelley. Of what *books* are these the very last words? The answers are on page 116.

1

So (said the doctor). Now vee may perhaps to begin. Yes?

2

And so I betake myself to that course, which is almost as much as to see myself go into my grave; for which, and all the discomforts that will accompany my being blind, the good God prepare me!

3

Come children, let us shut up the box and the puppets - for our play is played out.

4

The great shroud of the sea rolled on as it rolled 5,000 years ago.

5

'Lord!' said my mother, 'what is all this story about?' 'A Cock and Bull,' said - 'And one of the best of its kind I ever heard.'

6

It *was* a curious dream, dear, certainly - but now run in to your tea; it's getting late.

7

Cela est bien dit . . . mais il faut cultiver notre jardin.

8

Good grief - it's Daddy!

Of what films or shows are these the last lines?

9
It was beauty killed the beast.

10
The stuff that dreams are made of.

11
La commedia e finita.

12
Where the devil are my slippers, — ?

Of what characters in fiction are these the last lines?

13
A horse! A horse! My kingdom for a horse!

14
Floreat Etona.

15
I think I may go as far as to say, — that I have not lived wholly in vain.

16
Thus with a kiss I die.

17
Look, her lips. Look there, look there!

18
Done, because we are too menny.

Answers
And Yours I See Is Coming Down

1
Philip Roth, *Portnoy's Complaint*

2
Samuel Pepys, *Diary,* final entry, 31 May 1669 (in fact, he lived on until 1703)

3
Thackeray, *Vanity Fair*

4
Melville, *Moby Dick*

5
Sterne, *Tristram Shandy* (Yorick)

6
Lewis Carroll, *Alice's Adventures in Wonderland*

7
Voltaire, *Candide*

8
'Maxwell Kenton' (Terry Southern) and Mason Hoffenburg, *Candy*

9
King Kong

10
The Maltese Falcon (Bogart misquoting *The Tempest*)

11
Pagliacci

12

Pygmalion or *My Fair Lady* (Eliza)

13

Richard III in Shakespeare's play. The king's actual last words are said to have been: 'I will die king of England. I will not budge a foot . . . treason! Treason!'

14

Captain Hook in the stage version of J M Barrie's *Peter Pan*. In the book, he jeered 'bad form' and 'went content to the crocodile'.

15

Sherlock Holmes in Conan Doyle's *The Final Problem* (in last note to Dr Watson before plunging to his death with Professor Moriarty over the Reichenbach Falls).

16

Romeo in Shakespeare's play

17

King Lear in Shakespeare's play

18

The boy of Jude and Sue in Thomas Hardy's *Jude the Obscure*. He leaves this note before hanging himself and two other children.

They Couldn't Hit An Elephant
At This Dist____

General Sedgwick, a commander in the American Civil
War, is said to have met his end in 1864 with the above
words on his lips. It is left to few people to die saying words
worth handing down to posterity. Here are a few choice
examples from those who tried:

Am I dying or is this my birthday?

> *Nancy Astor, when all her
> children assembled by her
> deathbed, 1964*

I am about to - or I am going to - die: either expression is
used.

> *Dominique Bouhours,
> grammarian, 1702*

Quick, serve the dessert! I think I am dying!

> *Paulette Brillat-Savarin, sister
> of the gastronome Jean
> Anthelme Brillat-Savarin,
> said to have died on her
> 100th birthday.*

Take a step or two forwards, lads. It will be easier that
way.

> *Erskine Childers, Irish
> patriot, to firing squad, 1922*

And now, in keeping with Channel 40's policy of always
bringing you the latest in blood and guts, in living colour,
you're about to see another first - an attempted suicide.

> *Chris Chubbuck, TV news
> presenter, who shot herself
> on live TV, Sarasota, Florida,
> 1974*

I'm so bored with it all.

> *Winston Churchill, 1965*

Kiss me, Hardy.

The recording angel had to work overtime when Horatio Nelson laying dying on HMS Victory *at the Battle of Trafalgar, 1805. Did he say this or 'Kismet, Hardy' to his Flag Captain? Also: 'Thank God I have done my duty', 'Don't fling me overboard', and 'Take care of poor Lady Hamilton.'*

So here it is at last, the distinguished thing.

Henry James, 1916

Such is life.

Ned Kelly, outlaw, executed 1880.

See that Yul gets star billing. He has earned it.

Gertrude Lawrence, who died while starring in The King and I *with Yul Brynner, 1952*

Goodnight, my darlings, I'll see you tomorrow.

> *Sir Noel Coward, 1976*

That was a great game of golf, fellers.

> *Bing Crosby, 1977*

Thou liest!

> *'Posthumous' retort by Sir Everard Digby, hung, drawn and quartered for his part in the Gunpowder Plot, 1605, when the executioner plucked out his heart and said, 'Here is the heart of a traitor.'*

You have made three spelling mistakes.

> *Marquis de Fouras, to the officer who presented him with his death warrant, 1790*

Why fear death? Death is only a beautiful adventure.

> *Charles Frohman, who died when the* Lusitania *went down, 1915, quoting from* Peter Pan, *a play he once produced (Peter: 'To die will be an awfully big adventure.')*

If Mr Selwyn calls again, show him up; if I am alive I shall be delighted to see him, and if I am dead, he will be glad to see me.

> *Henry Fox, Lord Holland, of George Selwyn, who had a penchant for executions and corpses, 1840*

Stopped.

> *Joseph Henry Green, surgeon, feeling his own pulse, 1863*

It has all been very interesting.

> *Lady Mary Wortley Montagu, 1762*

Doctor: Your belly diminishes.
Thomas Paine: And yours augments.

> *1809*

Are you sure it's safe?

> *William Palmer, poisoner, on gallows, 1856*

This is not Beethoven lying here.

> *Schubert, 1828*

Tiens, je te reconnais de mes rêves. (Yes, I recognise you from my dreams.)

> *'Klop' Ustinov, to his son, Peter, 1962*

This wallpaper is killing me. One of us must go.

Oscar Wilde, 1900

Good! A woman who can fart is not dead.

Comtesse de Vercelis,
breaking wind on her
deathbed, 1728

Index

A

Agnew, Spiro 42
Albert, the Prince Consort 70
Alexander, Mrs Cecil Frances 53
Alice's Adventures in Wonderland 113, 116
All Authors are Equal 105
All Creatures Great and Small 51
Allen, Fred 19
Allen, Woody 112
All My Yesterdays 105
All Things Bright and Beautiful 53
American Declaration of Independence, The 22
Amin, Idi 73
Ancient Mariner, The 82, 84
Anderson, Kirk 9
Animal Crackers 29
Animal Farm 107, 108
Anka, Paul 81
Anne, H.R.H. Princess 93, 96
Annus Mirabilis 10
Antic Hay 17
Antony and Cleopatra 37, 93
Astor, Nancy 28, 119
Atlas, Charles 87, 89
Aubrey, John 11
Austen, Jane 14, 16, 50

B

Baden-Powell, Sir Robert 88
Bacon, Francis 18
Bagnold, Enid 9
Baldwin, Stanley 93, 96
Bankhead, Tallulah 24, 70
Barnes, Peter 73
Barnum, P.T. 19, 22
Barrie, J.M. 114, 117
Beckett, Samuel 128
Beecham, Sir Thomas 26
Beggar Man, Thief 53
Behan, Brendan 66
Benny, Jack 58
Bermudas 18
Bernhardt, Sarah 93
Bevan, Aneurin 26
Bevin, Ernest 29
Bhutto, Zulfiqar Ali, Prime Minister of Pakistan 76
Bible, The 22, 53, 106, 84, 90-2
Binyon, Laurence 84
Bogarde, Dirk 26, 58
Blunt, Alfred, Bishop of Bradford 94, 97
Bogart, Humphrey 30, 114, 116
Bolt, Robert 104
Bonaparte, Napoleon 23

Book of Common Prayer, The 22
Booth, John Wilkes 85, 88
Bouhours, Dominique 119
Braddock, Bessie 28
Brave New World 17
Bridge Too Far, A 104
Bridson, D.G. 28
Brillat-Savarin, Jean Anthelme 37
Brillat-Savarin, Paulette 119
British Expeditionary Force, The 41
British Sexual Offences Act, 1953 13
Brontë, Emily 58
Browning, Robert 52
Browning, Lieutenant-General Sir Frederick 106
Bryant, Anita 112
Brynner, Yul 120
Buchanan, James 98, 100
Buckman, Rob 26
Burgess, Anthony 51
Burke, Edmund 42
Burney, Fanny 50
Burton, Lady Isabel 74
Burton, Sir Richard 74
Butler, Samuel 13
Byron, Lord George 76
By the Pricking of my Thumbs 50

C

Campbell, Mrs Patrick 108, 111
Candide 113, 116
Candy 113, 116
Carlyle, Thomas 39, 41, 66
Carroll, Lewis 78, 113, 116
Carter, Jimmy 87, 89, 99, 100
Cartland, Barbara 27
Caruso, Enrico 37
Casablanca 55, 58
Casino Royale 15, 16
Cast a Cold Eye 50
Catcher in the Rye, The 14, 16
Cecilia 50
Cenci, The 113
Chamberlain, Neville 76, 89
Charles II 39, 41
Charles, H.R.H. Prince 39, 41, 85, 88, 93-4, 96-7
Chasen, Dave 30
Cherry Orchard, The 26
Chesterfield, Fourth Earl of 10
Chesterton, G.K. 15, 16, 43, 60, 90
Childers, Erskine 119
Chimes at Midnight 104
Christie, Agatha 50, 51, 75
Christie, Julie 58

Chronicles of Wasted Time 105
Chubbuck, Chris 119
Churchill, Randolph 28
Churchill, Winston 28, 41, 66, 75, 78, 93, 97, 100, 119
Cicero 22
Clooney, Rosemary 105
Cockburn, Claud 44
Colefax, Lady Sybil 29
Coleridge, Samuel Taylor 84
Colette 47
Colson, Charles W. 73
Complaint: Night Thoughts, The 22
Comus 106
Congreve, William 111
Contour, Mrs Jane 13
Coolidge, Calvin 98, 100
Cooper, Lady Diana 105
Cooper, Jilly 9
Coren, Alan 67
Country Wife, The 111
Coward, Noel 10, 22, 26, 28, 29, 30, 63, 76, 112, 121
Cowper, William 84
Crosby, Bing 39, 41, 121
Curran, John Philpott 23
Curzon, George Nathaniel 38, 40
Curzon, Marquess – of Kedleston 73

D

Darling 56, 58
Darrow, Clarence 98
Daudet, Alphonse 36
Davis, Bette 24
Davis, Sammy Jnr 76
Decline and Fall of the Roman Empire, The 50
Dickens, Charles 15, 16
Digby, Sir Everard 121
Dr Faustus 23
Dr Jekyll and Mr Hyde 26
Doyle, Sir Arthur Conan 40, 52, 114, 117
Dumas, Alexandre 87, 89
Du Maurier, Daphne 15, 16
Du Maurier, George 12

E

Edward II 17
Edward VII 94, 97
Edward VIII 94, 96, 97
Eichenlaub, John 12
Eisenhower, Dwight D. 98, 100
Eliot, T.S. 40
Elizabeth I 39, 41

" Acknowledgements "

Any compiler of quotation anthologies is indebted to a host of writers and speakers for his material. My thanks are due to all the people quoted in these pages, including the writers and publishers of the following books:

Barnes, Peter *The Ruling Class* (Heinemann, 1969)
Chesterton, G K *The Napoleon of Notting Hill* (Bodley Head, 1904)
Cooper, Jilly *Emily* (Arlington Books, 1975)
Du Maurier, Daphne *Rebecca* (Gollancz, 1938)

Isherwood, Christopher *Goodbye to Berlin* (Chatto & Windus, 1940)
Kenton, Maxwell *Candy* (Olympia Press, 1958)
Kipling, Rudyard *Selected Verse* (Penguin Books, 1977)
Larkin, Philip *High Windows* (Faber, 1974)
Milne A A *Winnie the Pooh* (Methuen, 1926)
Orwell, George *Animal Farm* (Secker & Warburg, 1945)
Orwell, George *Nineteen Eighty-Four* (Secker & Warburg, 1949)
Pepys, Samuel *The Diary of Samuel Pepys* (ed. Robert Latham

& William Matthews) (G Bell & Sons Ltd, 1970)
Pirsig, Robert M *Zen and the Art of Motorcycle Maintenance* (Bodley Head, 1974)
Roth, Philip *Portnoy's Complaint* (Jonathan Cape, 1969)
Saki *The Feast of Nemesis* (from *Beasts and Superbeasts,*) (John Lane, 1914)
Salinger, J D *The Catcher in the Rye* (Hamish Hamilton, 1951)
Sellar and Yeatman *1066 and All That* (Methuen, 1930)
Stoppard, Tom *Every Good Boy Deserves a Favour* (Faber, 1978)

Envoi

Vladimir: That passed the time.
Estragon: It would have passed in any case.
Vladimir: Yes, but not so rapidly.

> *Samuel Beckett,* Waiting for
> Godot